Paws to Reflect

Paws to Reflect

GODLY LESSONS BEST TAUGHT BY KITTENS

SHARI MEYER

BROOKSTONE
PUBLISHING GROUP
Birmingham, Alabama

Paws to Reflect

Brookstone Publishing Group
An imprint of Iron Stream Media
100 Missionary Ridge
Birmingham, AL 35242
IronStreamMedia.com

Library of Congress Control Number: 2023921329

Cover design by For the Muse Designs
Illustrations by Jennifer Schafer

ISBN: 978-1-960814-05-0 (paperback)
ISBN: 978-1-960814-06-7 (ebook)

1 2 3 4 5—28 27 26 25 24

Contents

Trusting

God's Plan

Discipline

Growing & Grace

Joy

God's Goodness

Preface

My husband and I started fostering in 2018, and we were hooked after our first group of kittens. The joy of watching our foster babies and moms find their personalities, overcome trauma or fears, and find their forever homes was incredibly rewarding for us.

These stories come from our experiences as foster parents for kittens and cats. Each cat or kitten name in this book was the real name of the feline that passed through our home; adopter names have been changed to protect their identity.

After our first year, we took a moment to consider, Where are we serving God in this? We knew we were serving a community, taking care of vulnerable animals, but what were we doing for God in all of this? So, we added the step of giving a small cat devotional book to each of our adoptive families. Whether they read the books or just put them in a giveaway box, we don't know, but we felt it was a way to share God's love in a gentle and kind way.

After a few years, the book was out of print and we could only purchase used copies. Some of the copies we purchased were not great quality and it felt discourteous giving them as gifts to forever families.

A friend suggested I write my own devotional, so I gave it a whirl and this book is the result. I hope you find these stories a reflection of God's love via tiny paws as our foster kittens and cats passed through our home and impacted our lives.

Acknowledgments

Thanks to the many hands that helped us see this book to publication.

Thanks to Kathy Schmidtke, who made the audacious suggestion that we should write our own devotional and seeded the possibility of actually making it happen. Thanks to Mary Lauck and James Walters who gave us first reads and edits. Thanks to my godson, Dirk Thayer, who entertained and toyed (briefly) with the technology and the grand idea that we could do our own illustrations using artificial intelligence. And grateful to Jennifer Schafer, artist extraordinaire, who created the illustrations when AI did not deliver.

Special thanks to my husband who patiently traveled this journey with me. He was instrumental in linking God's word and teachings to the foster experiences and pulling me out of the weeds when the stories got too long and the process became muddled.

Praise to God for showing us a way to share His word through the experience of fostering.

Trusting

Stirring & Purring

Curled on my lap,
you're no longer stirring.

As I pet you,
I can hear you purring.

I can tell you're almost sleeping,

But your little eyes keep peeking.

Close your eyes
and rest little one.

Tomorrow has time
for even more fun.

Not the Way We Hoped

*Trust in the LORD with all your heart
and lean not on your own
understanding.*

—Proverbs 3:5

Florala had five kittens that were about three weeks old when they arrived. After a few days, we were in love. The kittens were playful, cuddly, and so cute it shouldn't have been legal. Our first foster experience was off to a great start!

Two weeks later a red patch showed up on Vina's tummy, but she didn't seem bothered by it and was eating and playing just fine. Then a few days later La Fayette (aka FayFay) had a red patch above her eye. We took them to the shelter vet and the kittens were immediately diagnosed with ringworm! We had to return the whole litter to the shelter immediately. We were devastated.

We could see each one's personality, we had given them names, and we loved them; now we were faced with the reality that we had to send them back to shelter cages and nasty ringworm treatments. In addition to that, we were not allowed to foster for six months since our environment was "contaminated." It was not the vision we had of our first foster experience, it definitely did not go the way we hoped, but we could only trust that it would work out.

The kittens went through treatment, were adopted, and our house was only under quarantine for two months. We couldn't understand why all of this had to happen and with our first group of fosters too! We could have quit fostering, but by trusting God and not questioning WHY (for too long) we were encouraged to try again. Fortunately, we put our first foster fiasco behind us and went on to foster for many years with much joy!

May we always trust that the Lord is in control when the events in our lives are not going as we planned.

Watching and Waiting

Blessed are those who listen to me,
watching daily at my doors,
waiting at my doorway.

—Proverbs 8:34

We were on baby watch for the first time. We received our first pregnant cat to foster, and we were not well advised as to what to expect. We were told, "Momma kitties are really good at this, most of the time they will give birth at night and you won't even know until you see her."

Paullina, the momma-kitty-to-be, arrived and we set up a gentle night light. We created a birthing cave out of a cardboard box with big soft blankets draped over the top. We were ready. Now, when was Paullina going to be ready? Every night for thirteen nights we went to bed and told her we were ready for babies, hoping by morning she would have delivered her precious babies into this new life. We would sneak into her room and watch from the side; we would wait in her room hoping for something to happen. Nothing happened. She came to get lots of pets and rubs under her chin. She demanded tummy rubs, she purred, she waltzed around her room indifferent that anything was supposed to be happening.

Then on day fourteen she growled at us and went into the cave. A few minutes later, she came out and rubbed and loved on us. Something was up; the time was coming. At 11 a.m. she gave birth to her first kitten. It took another five hours to complete the process of bringing her babies into this world. The days and nights waiting and the long hours of delivery resulted in the blessing of five kittens.

We, too, can be blessed by listening, watching, and waiting for the Lord.

Plans to Prosper

"For I know the plans I have for you,"
*declares the L*ORD*, "plans to prosper you*
and not to harm you, plans to give you
hope and a future."

—Jeremiah 29:11

Odon's head looked bloody. Could he be adopted looking like that? During the forty-five-minute drive to the adoption event, he fought the carrier, banging his head and clawing to get out. More than one hundred people came to see kittens in a small venue where club music blared. People manhandled the kittens; it was miserable. Odon was filled with fear and cowered the entire time.

His brothers, Remington and Wayne, were quickly adopted, but I decided Odon just needed to go home. On the ride home, he was allowed out of the carrier to sit on my lap, but that was little consolation for a very hard day.

A man named Garrett heard about Odon because his sister had adopted Remington and Wayne at the event. He couldn't believe Odon was left behind without his brothers. Garrett then drove about an hour to meet with us and adopt Odon that very day!

Odon was an especially sensitive kitty and I couldn't help worrying most of the night about how Odon was doing. He had such a stressful day and now he would be alone after he had lived with other kittens.

In the morning, I received a text with a photo of Odon hanging out with his two brothers! Garrett and his sister decided it would be best for the boys to be together for a bit longer. What a nice surprise for us to receive a great photo of all three brothers together.

As difficult as that day started for Odon, in the end, the plan was designed for him to prosper and find his forever family.

We can be assured that God also has a plan for us to prosper, God wants us to be filled with hope and a blessed future.

Do Not Be Afraid

*Have I not commanded you? Be strong and courageous. Do not be afraid; do not be discouraged, for the L*ORD *your God will be with you wherever you go.*

—Joshua 1:9

Through the cat carrier viewing slot, five kittens looked at us and hissed. They arrived from Houston, Texas, with no mommy. Apparently, these kittens had been through some trauma and all five had upper respiratory infections and intestinal troubles. That's all we'll say about that, ugh.

After weeks of antibiotics and a lot of care, their health improved. The shelter suggested that to socialize these kittens we take them to a "yoga and kittens" event; we weren't convinced but followed the shelter's advice. What a disaster! The kittens were so fearful they wouldn't come out of the carrier and, although they had started to trust us, now the hissing resumed. This was no way to socialize kittens.

We started over. We worked with the kittens to build trust, and they began to show their personalities, grew in confidence, and showed lots of affection. Except for Darien—he could not be convinced. The trauma of his early days in Houston, the transport, and even the yoga event had settled deep in his psyche. He would hide as far under the couch or credenza as possible and cringe at any hand reaching to touch him.

Weeks of care and encouragement finally built his trust. Finally, the day came when he wouldn't cringe at a human's touch and would purr and lean into a chin rub. In uncertain situations he would still hesitate, but he was much stronger and courageous than when he first arrived.

In the same way, we can also set aside our fears and discouragement, trusting that God will be with us wherever we go.

Safety and Protection

For in the day of trouble
he will keep me safe in his dwelling;
he will hide me in the shelter of his
sacred tent and set me high upon a rock.

—Psalm 27:5

Brook finally had the green light to be adopted! Her six siblings had already found their forever homes. So, she was the only one left. Technical problems delayed her adoption posting for four days. Finally, Brook's adoption profile posted, and we eagerly waited for an adopter to find her but nothing happened. The next day, the director called to say all black kittens/cats were coming off the website because it was about two weeks until Halloween. We learned there are terrible people who do horrible things to black kittens during Halloween.

Brook seemingly would not have any chance for adoption for at least three more

weeks. We were disappointed but knew it was the right thing because Brook needed to be protected. We agreed to keep her posted on the website with a stipulation that she could not be adopted until after November 1.

Emmie, a previous adopter, sent a text message with a photo of Odon (Brook's brother) looking at Brook's posting online. Emmie and her siblings had been the recipients of Brook's brothers and now said that her mom, Malory, was so happy with how well the three kittens were doing that she wanted to adopt Brook for herself. Malory met, played with, and quickly fell in love with Brook.

We called the director requesting the adoption prior to November 1. This family already adopted three kittens with us, and they were obviously good people. Brook was allowed to go to her forever home that day! She was able to start her new life weeks earlier than expected where her forever family would provide her with all the safety, protection, and love she needed.

We can also be assured God will shelter us and keep us safe.

Trembling in Fear

Trembling in fear
as I reach for you.

So scared after what
you'd been through.

Now our job is
to make you feel safe,

Promising gentle hands
in this place.

Finally, you are safe
with us now.

Love and care is
our solemn vow.

Fear to Joy

I sought the Lord, and he answered me;
he delivered me from all my fears.

—Psalm 34:4

He couldn't stop shaking in fear. Payson hated cages, and he hated adoption events. He grew up with seven siblings and spent eight weeks knowing love and safety in his foster home.

Payson was sweet and affectionate, and his coloring was special as he was a faint tabby point Siamese. Yet, he was kind of a mess too. His fur was coarse, he had a black spot by his tear duct making his pretty face and blue eyes look like he had a gunky spot, and his voice was scratchy. We were sure he would be adopted quickly because he was simply an adorable mess.

We took him and his siblings to their first adoption event and set them in a row of cages at a pet store. Payson immediately started shaking in fear. As sweet as he was, no adopter could see it because he would cower and shake uncontrollably. It was horrible, not only for Payson but also for us! He did not get adopted that day or the next week either. Friends came to play with him, and he was adorable, so people weren't the problem; it was the cages and the scary environment.

Hours into the third adoption event a woman marched in and boldly announced, "I'm here for Payson. I will be adopting him today." Our hearts leaped! She saw his profile online and knew he was the kitten for her. Our hopes for a home for Payson were answered, and we knew he would not have to endure any more adoption events or cages.

In our own times of distress, we should seek God, and He will deliver us from all our fears.

You Will Have Enough

And my God will meet all your needs according to the riches of his glory in Christ Jesus.

—Philippians 4:19

Hayden was an adorable kitten with gray and white markings and much too big ears. He had a mask of gray around his eyes up through his ears with a cute white muzzle. He came to us with his three siblings at about five to six weeks old. They must not have had enough food because Hayden was very excited for food.

We mixed dry food soaked in a bit of water with wet cat food to make a slurry mixture. This was served in a large pie pan so all the kittens could gather around and eat. The others would take bites, but Hayden would shove his whole face into the food and suck it into his mouth making loud slurping sounds. The others would have their fill, walk away, and begin to lick their paws to clean up, but Hayden would just keep his face shoved in the food.

No matter how much he cleaned afterwards, or how much we cleaned him, his white muzzle always looked dirty because of his eating habits. So cute and yet always looking like a dirty mess. It was heartbreaking to try and reassure him that there would always be enough food, yet his experience told him that he couldn't be sure.

The entire time we had him, he never did outgrow the worry that he would have enough food. His food-stained muzzle was always a heartbreaking reminder of his inability to trust there would be enough.

Sometimes in life we have our own "food-stained muzzles" from not trusting that the Lord will provide.

Cat rescue is like a virus, . . . and once you're infected, it's incurable.

—Des Junior, *Rescue Ink: How Ten Guys Saved Countless Dogs and Cats, Twelve Horses, Five Pigs, One Duck, and a Few Turtles*

God's Plan

Sick Kittens

Sick kittens with upper
respiratory infections.

Nothing compared to what's
in those intestines.

These babies are creating
a big ol' mess.

Yet, how can I feel
anything but blessed.

Tiny kitten paws and
sweet little faces.

Getting you well puts me
through the paces.

Becoming Glorious

Who, by the power that enables him to bring everything under his control, will transform our lowly bodies so that they will be like his glorious body.

—Philippians 3:21

When it was time to nurse, Higley would get pushed away by the other stronger kittens. Higley was born into a big family with four boys and four girls. Eight kittens meant a lot of competition for everything.

The other kittens grew and their eyes opened, but Higley's right eye didn't fully open and stayed squinty. It looked like he was giving everyone the stink eye. He was smaller than the others, scrawny, and with that eye he was just kind of a mess. Adorable, but kind of a mess.

Duncan was one of Higley's brothers and had the same coloring. Duncan was the perfect kitten—strong, beautiful, perfectly proportioned, affectionate—he had it all. Higley, on the other hand, was getting bottle fed since he couldn't fight for enough milk, his squinty eye made him always seem cranky, and his back left paw had a white spot differentiating his appearance. Higley grew, got stronger, and his eye even lost its squint. It was time for an adoption event.

Chaos resulted with lots of people wanting to hold our kittens—it got a little crazy. A man asked me which kitten he was holding. I looked at the kitten and thought, *He is the perfect kitten, so muscular and strong, beautiful coloring, perfectly shaped face.* Then I looked at his right back paw, saw that distinctive white spot, and realized it was Higley (not Duncan)! The little kitten that was such a mess had grown into his own glory.

We may not start out being perfect, but in time, we, too, can come into our own glory with God's strength and love.

Could It Get Worse?

And we know that in all things God works for the good of those who love him, who have been called according to his purpose.

—Romans 8:28

Carrabelle was an orange tabby, and she grew to be a strong, sweet girl with lots of love to offer. She was adopted by Laurie at a pet store event. Laurie took over an hour to decide but concluded Carrabelle was the right kitten for her and her young son. Days later, Laurie called saying she couldn't keep Carrabelle because her son was allergic to her. She shared pictures of her son cuddling with Carrabelle. They were both heartbroken.

Laurie went to the shelter to talk about returning Carrabelle and was horrified that Carrabelle would be placed in a small metal cage. Laurie asked if we would take

Carrabelle back instead of having to put her in a cage. We quickly agreed and said we would gladly resume fostering. The shelter rejected the request. They required Carrabelle be put in a cage at the shelter. We were devastated and feared Carrabelle would not do well because she was so social.

To make things worse, a snowstorm shut down everything for days, which meant Carrabelle was alone in a metal cage with no chance for adoption. As feared, she did not do well; she fell ill, and the shelter decided to move her to another foster family for more care. We were discouraged that we still weren't allowed to care for her.

In the end, Carrabelle responded to medication, bonded to another kitten at the other foster home, and was adopted as a bonded pair with her new kitty friend. As painful and distressing as the situation turned, all things worked out for good.

We, too, can know that God works for the good of those who love Him.

Knows the Heart

But the L<small>ORD</small> said to Samuel, "Do not consider his appearance or his height, for I have rejected him. The L<small>ORD</small> does not look at the things people look at. People look at the outward appearance, but the L<small>ORD</small> looks at the heart."

—1 Samuel 16:7

Rosston meowed sadly when he was scared. He was insecure and shied away from all people. He wasn't a kitten that wanted to be held, and he was the last kitten in his family still waiting to find a forever home.

Although he had already endured two other adoption events, here he was again at his third. Rosston wasn't doing well having people poke their fingers in at him and trying to touch him in a cage hour after hour. This looked like another hard day for all of us.

Morgan and his mom came to see the kittens. Morgan was about two and a half years old. Morgan spied Rosston and pointed to him and wanted to hold him. I got Rosston out of the cage and held Rosston for Morgan, and he petted and talked to him. Rosston was not secure and cried quite a lot during this time. I told Morgan's mom that there were a number of really nice kittens at the event today and I'm sure they could find just the right kitty for Morgan.

After twenty minutes, they returned to us and Morgan insisted on seeing Rosston again. I told Morgan's mom, "Rosston is just a bit insecure." Her response was, "Well, so is someone else," nodding to Morgan. From the bits of conversations, I understood that there was a family separation in process. Morgan was clear that this was the kitty for him even though the adults measured the outward appearance.

Maybe Morgan could see the heart of a kitty and it matched his own, just as the heart of God knows our heart.

Tiny to Mighty

A lion, mighty among beasts,
who retreats before nothing.

—Proverbs 30:30

Oh my, she was so tiny. Kayenta, aka KK, was part of a litter of eight kittens. She was the only orange kitten in this group, and some say female orange tabbies are uncommon. We might debate that as we've had a number of orange tabby girls in our foster experience, but that doesn't make KK any less exceptional.

She demonstrated toughness right away, and when the wrestling matches would begin (there are always wrestling matches with her seven siblings), she would not stand back. She would hold her ground with any of her siblings. However, when it came to getting enough to eat, she was just too small and always got pushed away while the others nursed heartily.

She became one of the bottle babies needing supplemental milk to help her keep growing at a good pace.

Soon she was eating wet and dry food and, although still small, didn't need any extra help to keep pace. The time came for adoption; we spent an exhausting day at an event and KK was the last kitten left. The shelter wanted to take her back where she would be put in a metal cage, and although we knew her chances for adoption were greater there, we were horrified at the thought of her in a cage.

With only fifteen minutes left, a nice couple adopted KK! Later, they sent us a picture of her lying across a huge dog completely at home as if saying, "This is my dog." Although she started out tiny, she truly grew to be mighty.

May we also grow to be mighty and retreat from nothing that God calls us to do.

Pet Store Cages

I hate to see you
in the pet store cage,

Praying a family picks you today.

I'd much prefer
you were in my lap,

Curled up, comfy, taking a nap.

But we must endure
the pet store cage.

Sadly, it's the adoption
agency's way.

Crushed in Spirit

*The LORD is close to the brokenhearted
and saves those who are crushed
in spirit.*

—Psalm 34:18

His beautiful life was gone. Nothing remained but crushing pain, and my heart was broken. Fifteen hours earlier, he had arrived with his mom and five siblings. From the moment he came out of the carrier, we could tell that something wasn't right.

We called the shelter and explained that he wasn't moving well, and there was much worry. The shelter said to watch and wait. He was given antibiotics earlier; that was all the action the shelter would take. Two hours later, he hadn't eaten or taken a drink and his movements were terribly slow. Our worry and fear increased, and we called the emergency care line. They were not helpful and didn't offer additional care or support. Each time we checked on him, our worry amplified. At one point, we found him at the water dish and some hope emerged. Morning came and, to our relief, he had lived through the night.

Before anyone was "officially operating," desperate calls were made telling the shelter that he needed the first vet appointment immediately. We waited for a response. At 7 a.m., his mom gave him a cleaning lick on his head, and he gave out a small cry. I gathered him in my arms, watched his breath stop, and wept.

We drove him to the shelter wrapped in a soft towel; wrapped in love. His tiny body without life, without spirit. I was crushed by the loss. The shelter wanted a name for him, so I named him Bonifay, which means *bon enfant* or "good baby." In time, the grief of losing this "good baby" lightened, but even years later tears fall.

Healing rests in knowing the Lord sees our broken hearts and saves our crushed spirits.

The smallest feline is a
masterpiece.

—Leonardo da Vinci

Discipline

More Work to Be Done

Kitty litter scattered everywhere.

Fighting over food
you were supposed to share.

Low growls and
mean little hisses.

Stop the fighting—
she's your sister!

More work to be done
on their social skills.

No biting and scratching
we try to instill.

Thankfully naptime
is a small reprieve.

When they awake, who knows
what's up their paw-sleeve.

Sneaky Pee-er

You, God, know my folly;
my guilt is not hidden from you.

—Psalm 69:5

Aubrey was an especially pretty orange tabby, a bit lighter coloring around her face with sparkling blue eyes, she was one to steal hearts. But Aubrey also had a sneaky side. She came in our second group of foster kittens, just five adorable orange tabby kittens.

We placed a comforter on the floor so the kittens would have a warm, soft place to sit or sleep off the tile floor. In another area, there was a space for their litter boxes, food, and water. One day, Aubrey's brother went to a spot on the comforter and started to scratch as if he was covering something up. We checked and didn't see or smell anything. Then another kitten scratched the same area. These kittens were trying to tell us something, but we had not quite figured it out.

Then it happened. Aubrey casually walked over to a corner of the comforter, barely squatted down, and started to pee. No scratching, no preparing, just a very sneaky pee. Most times she used the litter box just fine, but for no reason, she would go to the corner of the comforter and barely squat down to do her sneaky pee. We got better at sensing her "indiscretion mode" and quickly relocated her to the litter box. In time, she stopped her sneaky behavior, but it took a watchful eye.

She thought she could hide her folly, but her siblings would not accept her sneaky behavior so with their sensitive noses and our vigilance Aubrey changed her ways.

Let us be mindful that none of us can hide our indiscretions from God. Let us ask for forgiveness and the strength to do what is right.

For Your Own Good

*Blessed is the one whom God corrects;
so do not despise the discipline of
the Almighty.*

—Job 5:17

Tazlina's soft mewing was coming from behind the closed door. She wanted us to open that door. She paused for a bit then tried mewing louder and still we did not open the door. Then we said to her, "You can only come out if you have good behavior."

Tazlina loved to be with people, and we loved her. She was a singleton and was eager to be with people. Most of the time she was a very good kitten, but sometimes she would forget her manners and she would bite. Not a bite to draw blood, just bad behavior. She didn't yet understand biting was not OK for a proper little girl kitten. She did not grow up with siblings who easily teach each other that biting is not good behavior and bad consequences come as a result.

Other kittens respond with a returned bite, a paw swipe, a yelp, or simply leaving and not playing anymore. Since Tazlina didn't have any siblings, she would hear the word "Ow!" loudly every time she bit and then she would be placed in a room behind a closed door without people. Sometimes "Ow!" and isolation happened over and over and over, but it was the only way we knew to teach her that certain behavior was not OK and needed correction. We never allowed anger to influence any of the discipline, just a heartfelt endeavor to correct behavior so love could flourish.

The same is true with God: His correction is never for hurt or harm but rather designed so that we can live in a way to love abundantly and be loved completely.

Do Not Lead Astray

Whoever heeds discipline shows
the way to life,
but whoever ignores correction
leads others astray.

—Proverbs 10:17

Anita had a special talent that we had never seen before in a mommy kitty. She could open cupboard doors, and she loved dark places to explore. This presented quite the problem because the space for her and her three kittens was in a master bathroom. Eleven cupboards enclosed bathroom supplies and the plumbing for the jetted tub. Gaps and holes under the tub allowed for the plumbing that led under the subflooring. A scary place for a mommy kitty but a horribly dangerous place for a small kitten. Anita started by pulling at the bottom of the cupboard door around the jetted tub. We would gently tell her no, and she would leave it alone, but as we would learn, not for long!

Anita and the three kittens were left alone for about an hour. When we returned to the room, all we could find were two kittens. Immediate panic! Where were Anita and Rigby, her little boy? Then it struck us—the cupboard! Anita, who would not heed our gentle discipline, had opened the cupboard door and, worst of all, led Rigby into danger.

We found Rigby close to the cupboard door and snatched him fast. Anita was in the recesses of the space, exploring, and having a grand time. We eventually retrieved her. The fear of what could have happened to Rigby spurred drastic action. Large boxes were filled with many heavy books and placed in front of every cupboard. As strong and determined as she was, she was never able to get into the cupboards again.

May all of us accept discipline and correction so that we may live with blessings and never lead others astray or into harm.

Defiant Nature

*Do not remember the sins of my youth
and my rebellious ways;
according to your love remember me,
for you, L*ORD*, are good.*

—Psalm 25:7

Defiant. Maybe she was just born that way. She was so beautiful, Taylor the soft gray kitten with adorable eyes and the sweetest face. But that girl was defiant!

A lamp sat on a table in the room—one place the kittens were not allowed to go. Every other inch of the room was perfectly acceptable for play, sleep, wrestling, anything a kitten could dream up! All the kittens knew from the loud snap of fingers and the harsh word *no* that being on the table with the lamp was not allowed. All the other kittens minded without fuss, but not Taylor. That girl would climb on that table and hit the pull chains until they

rang out with a clattering sound of metal on metal.

One day I was cleaning in the room next door. When I walked into the room, there Taylor sat on the table with the lamp looking right at me. She knew she shouldn't be there. I stared her down and told her "No" and made a loud snap of my fingers. She didn't move; she didn't even blink. Instead, she looked right at me and swiped at the pull chain ringing out the loud metal-on-metal clank once again.

She was simply defiant and nothing was going to stop that girl from doing what she wanted. Nothing short of physically picking her up, putting her in another room, and removing the lamp was going to stop her.

Sometimes our own defiance can also cost us the light. When we find ourselves in defiance, we should ask the Lord to forgive our rebellious ways and remember us according to His love.

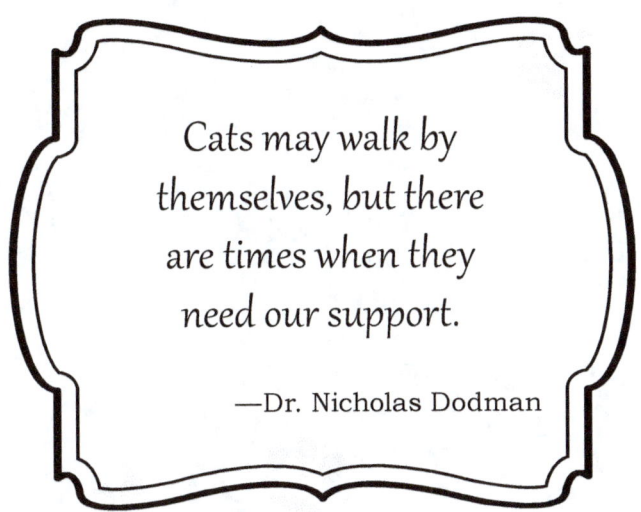

Cats may walk by themselves, but there are times when they need our support.

—Dr. Nicholas Dodman

Growing & Grace

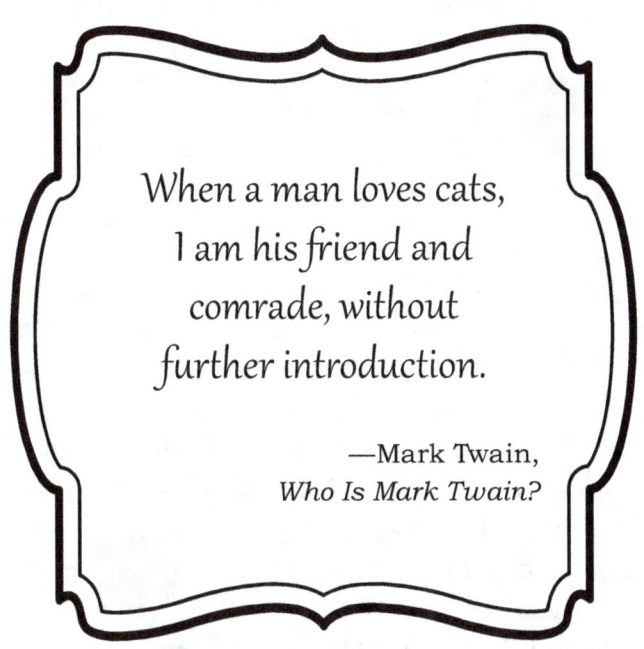

When a man loves cats,
I am his friend and
comrade, without
further introduction.

—Mark Twain,
Who Is Mark Twain?

All in Patience

Therefore, as God's chosen people,
holy and dearly loved, clothe yourselves
with compassion, kindness, humility,
gentleness and patience.

—Colossians 3:12

He was so much bigger than the rest of them. It was obvious Dayton wasn't really part of this litter. He got mixed into a group of kittens and was now growing up with six unrelated siblings. Dayton was affectionate and perfected a move we dubbed "the Dayton Flop." He would climb up on a person's lap and flop over to have his head held and chin rubbed. He would then cuddle in for the perfect nap.

His sister Riley was one of the smallest in the litter, and she was a cutie. She also showed signs that she was too young to be taken from her mom and would desperately seek out something to suckle. Her favorite item to suckle turned out to be Dayton's toes on his back foot. As naptime would approach, the kittens would find their comfy spots to settle in and Riley would seek out Dayton's toes.

Although Dayton wasn't really her brother, he showed incredible gentleness and patience with his "stepsister" and let her suckle until she would fall into a peaceful sleep. Sometimes he would look embarrassed, even a bit mortified, that his stepsister was sucking on his toes, but with compassion he would let her stay.

Being so much bigger than she was, he could have easily pushed her away and found a different place for his own nap, but the love in his character allowed him to put his pride away and let his baby stepsister find the comfort she craved.

All of us can strive to live full of compassion, kindness, humility, gentleness, and patience.

Speak Truthfully

Therefore each of you must put off falsehood and speak truthfully to your neighbor, for we are all members of one body.

—Ephesians 4:25

Riley had a black head, black tail, white body, and one perfect spot on her left side. She was compact and had a cuteness that was off the charts. She had six siblings, so she knew a lot about playing hard and standing her ground. She did not show a lot of affection to people, but she wasn't fearful or hissy. She was best described as indifferent and aloof.

Carl expressed interest in meeting Riley and possibly adopting her. We were truthful with him that she was not a cuddly personality. She liked rubs and purred but only when she picked and definitely not on a person's lap. We also let Carl know that she showed some insecurity and needed to suckle. At the time, her older brother's foot was serving as the suckling device. Carl would need to find an alternative to give her the comfort she needed.

We tried to be clear that she had a few eccentricities that Carl would need to work through if he adopted Riley. Since adopting a kitten can be a twenty-or-more-year commitment, we wanted him to know the truth about her. Carl spent a lot of time with Riley, and we believed she would have more affection to share over time, but no promises were made. Riley would be Riley. We wanted to speak truthfully since we all wanted Riley to have the best fit in her forever home.

Sometimes pointing out issues can be difficult, but speaking truth with a caring heart always has the best outcome and benefits those around us.

Spinning and Spinning

Therefore I do not run like someone running aimlessly; I do not fight like a boxer beating the air.

—1 Corinthians 9:26

She had to be all alone with no other kittens around for it to happen. Finding that opportune time wasn't easy with six other kittens running around and growing up. Riley was an especially small girl with a black tail, a black head, a white body, and one perfect circle on her left side. She was also built very compact. She was no pushover though; she could hold her own with any of her siblings, and her personality was developing to show a strong independent side.

She was up on the shower bench, no easy feat to accomplish with as compact and small as she was, and she was spinning in circles. Round and round and round.

Starting at the right side next to the wall, she would start spinning and only go one direction, round and round. She would spin across the entire length of the bench all the way across until she touched the wall on the other side. We weren't sure if she was chasing her tail or a shadow or what was going on, but she would just spin and spin.

As silly as it seems, with no reason or purpose in her moves, she just spun her way from one side to the other. Although it was cute to watch, it was so pointless. We could not understand why she felt the need to spin or why she would only do it when she thought no one was watching.

Watching a kitten, someone else, or even ourselves spin aimlessly might be amusing, but God calls us to pursue Him and avoid running aimlessly without purpose.

Can't Be Sad

I've said it before
and I'll say it again:

I can't be sad
when I play with a kitten.

Seeing you chase a sibling
or pounce on toys,

I'm delighted to watch you
bursting with joy.

A kitten's play is
rambunctious and crazy;

It's over the top
fun and amazing.

All for the Kittens

Commit to the Lᴏʀᴅ whatever you do,
and he will establish your plans.

—Proverbs 16:3

After our first year of fostering kittens, we were hooked on fostering and had also found a way to serve God by adding a devotional gift for each forever family. We loved giving kittens a safe and nurturing place to grow up until they could find their forever home.

Some kittens came from terrible situations; most of the time we didn't know their story but could tell from their fear, distress, or physical condition that they had endured trauma. Entrusted with these tiny lives, we committed to do everything in our power in the best interest of our foster kittens. The kittens always took first priority for us.

On occasions we would disagree with shelter staff on some of their protocols.

They had priorities of making money and moving merchandise (the kittens); we had a single priority of putting the best interest of the kittens first. Unfortunately, after several significant differences of opinion about how the kittens should be managed, we were informed that the staff decided it would be better if we no longer fostered with their shelter.

We weren't really surprised, but it still hurt to be fired from a volunteer job. We loved fostering kittens, we loved helping little lives thrive, and we wanted to help. Weeks later, we found a smaller rescue organization, and after lengthy talks with the executive director and full disclosure that we had been fired from the big animal shelter, she readily took us as volunteers and we were fostering kittens again. We foster kittens believing it is where we can serve God and our community, and even though we faced difficulty our plans were not derailed.

When it seems we are at an end, God has already designed a way forward.

Big Baby

I gave you milk, not solid food, for
you were not yet ready for it. Indeed,
you are still not ready.

—1 Corinthians 3:2

Felton was different in lots of ways from all his siblings. So tiny and adorable with his big blue eyes, fluffy-long hair, and the only kitten with Siamese coloring, he was irresistible. As adorable as he looked, he was also a big baby.

When his siblings were racing around playing hard and chasing one another, he would nap. When he played, he wasn't focused and would just meander. No purpose, no intent, just a lot of ambling for Felton. The most challenging phase of his babyhood was when he refused to eat kitten food. He insisted on only nursing. His siblings would gobble up kitten food, and Felton would look for his mommy. Laurel

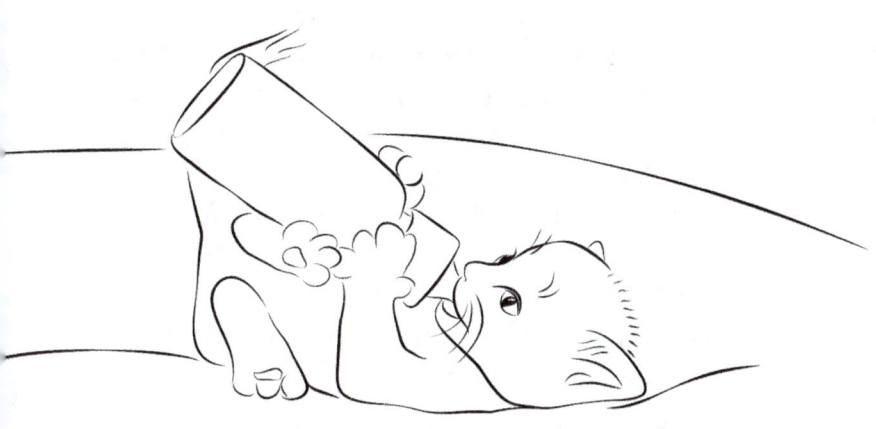

was a really good mommy, but she reached a point when she just wasn't having anymore of Felton nursing; she would kick him away or walk away. The time had come for him to grow up and eat solid food.

Felton pestered her, but she would not let him nurse. He started to lose weight, so we started feeding him with a syringe filled with Kitten Replacement Milk (KRM). In a few days we migrated to mixing the KRM with wet food, yet he still refused to eat from a bowl. Weeks of working with him convinced him he must stop being a big baby and eat solid food. Cuteness was easy, but growing up was very hard for Felton.

We each may have things we want to hang on to in our own lives that keep us from becoming mature, but like Felton a time comes when we must stop behaving like babies and grow into the life God designed for us.

Growing in Confidence

So do not fear, for I am with you;
do not be dismayed, for I am your God.
I will strengthen you and help you;
I will uphold you with my righteous
right hand.

—Isaiah 41:10

Pono needed that raggedy old toy mouse to strengthen and encourage him. The mouse, once a cute toy, long ago lost its tail, its eyes, and its nose. I restitched the toy to hold the stuffing inside; nothing left but a blue, fuzzy, stuffed orb. Yet that raggedy blue mouse was just what Pono needed.

Pono was a gray stripy boy kitty with an affectionate and fun personality. He had five siblings, two of which looked just like him. These kittens were taken away from their mom too early causing several of them to need to suckle, but none more so than Pono. He quickly latched on to the

worn-out blue mouse and would position it between his paws so he could knead on it and suckle on it until he fell asleep.

The insecurity of being taken from his mom too soon caused him to seek out comfort almost with desperation. Over time he started to be more confident and didn't need to suckle as much, but occasionally he still wanted the raggedy blue mouse. When the time came to be adopted, we sent the blue mouse with him and his new family so that he could be strengthened as he worked through the transition to his new home. We hoped that no new insecurities would surface, but he had his blue mouse to rely on, if required.

When life is uncertain and our own insecurities surface, we might feel like we need a blue mouse like Pono, but we can rely on God who will strengthen and help us.

Broken Rules

*These rules, which have to do with
things that are all destined to perish
with use, are based on merely human
commands and teachings.*

—Colossians 2:22

Five kittens were ready, and we were off to
our first adoption event at the pet store. It
was time for our foster kittens to find their
forever homes. The place was packed with
people, and a young woman asked about
Benson. Benson was an adorable little boy
kitty with black and white markings and a
perfectly placed mustache.

The woman called her friend and said,
"He is perfect, you need to get down here."
Tammy arrived and spent time meeting
Benson, holding him, and was convinced
he was the right kitty for her. Her cat had
passed away several months prior, and
it had taken time for her to move beyond

the grief. Now she was ready for a kitten. She mentioned that it was a major event weekend with her work, and she would be gone for about sixteen hours each day. She didn't want to take Benson home to leave him alone, so she asked if we could hold him until Tuesday and she would pick him up then. I readily agreed.

I was wrong. There were rules with the shelter, and this was not allowable. I had broken the rules! In my defense, I had not been told the rules and simply acted to make a perfect match happen. The shelter fought hard to not allow the adoption, but I fought harder, and they finally acquiesced. I understood that the shelter had liabilities they needed to manage, and once I was informed of the rules, I did not break them again.

The shelter issued human commands and sometimes it's important to see and act beyond the rules to enable things that endure like love, devotion, and gratitude.

Joy

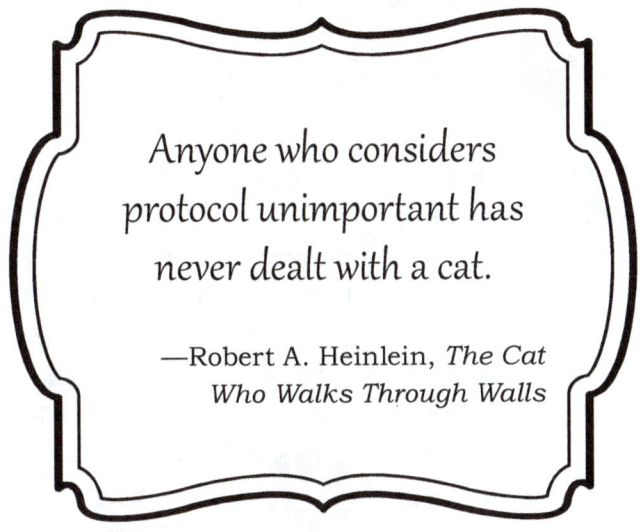

Anyone who considers protocol unimportant has never dealt with a cat.

—Robert A. Heinlein, *The Cat Who Walks Through Walls*

Finding Rest

Yes, my soul, find rest in God;
my hope comes from him.

—Psalm 62:5

My husband's six-foot, lanky body stretched out on the tile floor with his head propped against the cabinet. It didn't look very comfortable, but he was breathing softly in a light sleep. Savannah, a gorgeous six-week-old Siamese kitten was lying on his chest, right at the top of his ribcage. Savannah's curled body rose and fell with each of his breaths.

Although there were a variety of kitty beds and soft blankets scattered around the room, this was Savannah's favorite place to sleep. In all honesty, napping with Savannah was a favorite for my husband too. A kitten sleeping on his chest felt like peace and love wrapped into one.

She reached one paw out in a tiny stretch and curled it under her chin as they rhythmically breathed together. Resting deeper, the two of them slept until his breath started to become a little louder, almost a snore, but not quite. Savannah rolled over and put her paw over her eyes. Later she scooted up higher on his chest and tried to curl up but quickly decided sleep time was over.

She stood up, gave a little stretch, and walked right toward his face as his breathing got just a bit louder. Her paw pushed on his collar bone and he awoke to the beautiful kitten face of Savannah looking him straight in his eyes. Savannah was awake, and she was sure everyone was rested and that it was indeed time to play, or at least eat a snack.

In lives filled with busy schedules and unrelenting demands, finding rest in God will restore our hope in Him and give us peace.

Filled with Awe

The whole earth is filled with awe
at your wonders;
where morning dawns, where
evening fades,
you call forth songs of joy.

—Psalm 65:8

There really wasn't much happening. There wasn't a lot of action—some twitches but not much to see; yet the hours would pass, and I would sit in awe and watch five kittens in their first days of life. Newborn kittens aren't really that cute. Candidly, they look more like little rats than the fuzzy, adorable, calendar photo kittens we all know and love. Yet, they were captivating me.

Spellbound, I watched:

- tiny ears twitch as they nursed;
- tongues no bigger than a grain of rice dart in and out searching to nurse;

- spindly legs stretch and push toward just the right place to nurse;
- feet grasping with tiny claws already formed at the end of their toes;
- tiny bodies snuggle into mom kitty to stay warm during a nap.

Mom kitty would clean a baby, and sometimes her tongue was so rough that the kitten would just be flipped to a new location. Little bodies would flop awkwardly after tumbling from a nursing spot or from a momma kitty stretch as she got more comfortable. The kittens' bodies were rather spindly, so they didn't roll, they just tumbled to a new spot. They had no impressive body control or purposeful action, yet they were perfectly formed creations that mesmerized for hours.

Most surprising was how much happiness and joy came from just being with these babies and watching them. We watched them do "not much" and yet the time was filled with delight and wonder. In a tiny cardboard box with five newborn kittens, the wonders of God were so beautifully displayed that joy and awe filled the world.

Return the Joy

*How can we thank God enough for you
in return for all the joy we have in the
presence of our God because of you?*

—1 Thessalonians 3:9

Our kittens sat in cages; people poked at them but few were getting adopted. It was turning into a long, hard day. I could see my husband across the way, and he was talking to a very attractive young woman, and they were both smiling and laughing. I, in all honesty, started to get a little annoyed.

My husband brought her over then, and she introduced herself. She had been doing yard work but remembered she had to get cat food, so she dashed over to the pet store. She saw the signs at the front for the adoption event, so on the off chance, she came back to see if we were there.

A year earlier, she adopted one of our kittens, and there was a big issue with promises that I made to her, which broke a bunch of the shelter's rules. It all worked out, but it was definitely memorable for all of us. She adopted Benson, gave him the new name of Hank, and was here to tell us that he was amazing. She showed us videos of him pouting because she had to leave for work and him fetching a toy over and over. The love between the two of them was undeniable.

On a difficult day with not a lot of adoptions, how could we thank her enough for sharing such joy! Because of her willingness to look for us and share her happiness, the day turned out to be more memorable than the day she adopted our Benson, now her Hank. Let us bring joy to others in ways that overwhelm them with gratitude.

Time to Dance

You turned my wailing into dancing;
you removed my sackcloth and
clothed me with joy.

—Psalm 30:11

Anna's personality was growing each day, and we could see that she was a spunky and stubborn little girl living up to the true Tortoiseshell or "Tortie" reputation. Torties are known to be strong-willed, and the term *tortitude* is widely known in the cat world.

Most of the time, Anna's tortitude showed up by the amount of time she refused to come out from under the couch. She would play with her siblings, and she would nap relaxed in the room, but when a stranger came in—*whoosh*—she would hide, acting fearful and difficult. A mom and her teenage daughter came to meet Anna and were considering adopting her. We decided the

best course of action was to keep Anna in the room where there was no couch where she might try to hide.

When the adopters came, they sat on the floor, and Anna wandered around them checking everything out. Anna didn't run and hide, but she didn't greet the visitors with much affection either. They asked if Anna had any favorite toys, and we showed them that if we dropped a dry food kibble on the floor, Anna would bat it, hop, and dance around it like crazy. They were completely captivated by this adorable girl dancing for all her might around a dry food kibble. Anna played with that piece of kibble for ten minutes and the adopters' hearts were completely lost to her.

Even though Anna would hide a lot and at times we considered her especially stubborn, she also showed us that she could dance for joy. When we trust God, He can turn our difficulties into dancing and joy.

Found the Cure

Resting against my chest,
I can feel the purr.

Stress is gone,
I have found the cure.

This kitten is filled
with contentment and trust.

This is a great spot;
I may never get up.

Tiny purrs and a restful sleep.

This is where love
and serenity meet.

Full-On Love Affair

You know you are
loved and adored.

Even scooping your poo
isn't really a chore.

I'm glad to be
in charge of your care.

Yes, this is a full on love affair.

God's Goodness

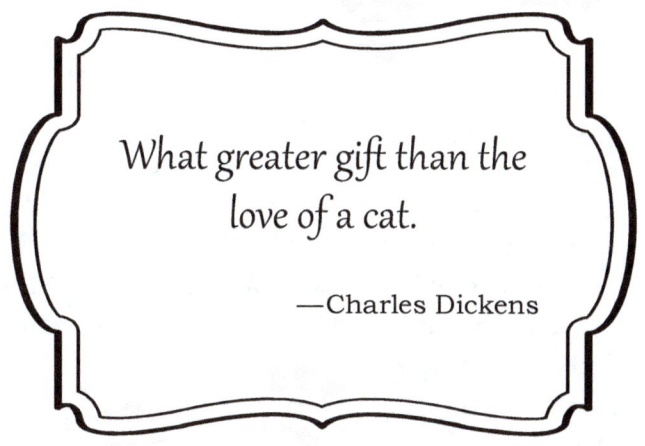

What greater gift than the
love of a cat.

—Charles Dickens

More Than Expected

*You crown the year with your bounty,
and your carts overflow with
abundance.*

—Psalm 65:11

The shelter advised us that Tigger was due to give birth at any moment. We were ready to receive her and her litter of kittens as soon as it was safe to transfer her and the babies. Just four days after the kittens were born, the shelter told us it was time to transport them and we would take over the care.

We heard something about a big litter, maybe six, but still weren't aware of how many would be coming to our care. Arriving at the shelter, we found that Tigger and the kittens had already been tucked into a carrier. We signed pages of paperwork, picked up supplies, and headed out the door. As we were leaving, a shelter person said something about "eight." We thought, *Yikes, seven kittens and Tigger the mom.*

Once home, we gently placed the carrier with Tigger and the babies in the master bathroom; this would be their new home for about the next twelve weeks. Not wanting to create more stress, we removed the door to the carrier so Tigger knew she was free. She could decide when she was ready to come out. Seeing her and the kittens would have to wait until she was ready to venture out.

We opened the paperwork and were reading the stats on the kittens—weights, coloring, gender—and that's when the shock hit: four boys, four girls, *and* a mom! My goodness this was a huge litter! More than expected or anticipated and yet each one a gift and a treasure.

Even in surprises, the best thing to do is to give thanks when life overflows with abundance.

Gifts from Above

Every good and perfect gift is from above, coming down from the Father of the heavenly lights, who does not change like shifting shadows.

—James 1:17

Tigger came to us with her eight babies, and she was a great mommy. However, with that many kittens, three babies were not putting on weight or growing as quickly as the others. We saw that KK (Kayenta), Marana, and Higley were just getting pushed away by the bigger kittens and didn't have enough might to win a spot to nurse. Something had to be done. Enter "The Milkman."

My husband took to bottle feeding these three to add to their nourishment. KK and Marana would continue to wrestle for a place to nurse until they would be plucked away and a bottle put in their tiny mouths.

They easily filled their tummies from the bottle without any struggle while "The Milkman" held them close.

Higley viewed the situation a bit differently. When all the kittens would be wrestling for a place to nurse, and Higley saw my husband come in the room, he would run as fast as his little legs could carry him to "The Milkman." He knew he could eat to his heart's content and did not have to wrestle for his nourishment.

He didn't stop trying to nurse with his mom, but he also knew that there was one providing perfect gifts from above just for him. He watched faithfully for "The Milkman" and ran to him with expectations that he would receive exactly what he craved the most.

As Higley trusted and looked for "The Milkman," we can all the more trust in a loving God who provides us with every perfect gift.

Preparing for You

And if I go and prepare a place for you,
I will come back and take you to be with
me that you also may be where I am.

—John 14:3

Watson, a Siamese boy kitty, was part of a litter of four kittens that came from Houston. Although what happened in their first seven weeks of life is unclear, they certainly experienced distressing things. Some time passed before they could trust and give affection, but once they knew they were safe and loved, they thrived.

Watson never did trust being carried. He would squirm, wiggle, scratch, and fight to get free. He just wanted to be put down to the floor where he was completely in control. We used a technique called a "purrito" where he got wrapped up tight in a towel so he couldn't fight, then we could carry him if needed.

A family was interested in adopting Watson. Their eleven-year-old daughter begged unrelentingly for a pet; however, they had never before owned a pet. The daughter saw Watson online and was convinced he was her kitten; her parents finally agreed. The parents did not have experience with kittens but were wise and asked many questions and meticulously prepared for the arrival of a new family member.

The mom asked various questions, including proper litter box and cat carrier sizes. They were keen to know what toys, beds, scratching posts, dishes, food, treats, and so on would be best. They invested a lot of time and energy preparing for Watson's arrival, ensuring everything would be perfect for him. Watson's forever family was taking him to be with them in a place that was perfectly prepared and where they would be together.

We can also look forward to a perfectly prepared place in heaven when we are called to our forever home with God.

Mews & News

Who could have guessed that
these kitten's gentle mews

Would be such a powerful force
to deliver God's news?

Lessons of resolve, joy, and hope,

Wisdom lifting us up
or helping to cope.

What a gift to receive
kitten nose kisses

And more joy to know
God hears prayers and wishes.

Proclaim All That Has Been Done

Give praise to the LORD, proclaim
his name;
make known among the nations
what he has done.

—Psalm 105:1

We have a naming protocol where each group of fosters is given names from cities or places in a state. Alphabetically this group's names were from the state of Delaware. Rodney Village has about thirteen hundred residents, and the name Rodney reminded us of Rodney Dangerfield—who talked a lot!

Rodney seemed like the perfect name for this gray stripy boy with white paws that came to us from Houston with his mom and five siblings. He had a perfectly shaped face with white cheeks, chin, and chest. He was really so cute we couldn't help but snuggle with him.

Right away we noticed that Rodney was not shy about voicing his opinions. He would let us know just what he thought about everything. He was never insistent, but he was always available with a meow to let us know his thoughts on the subject. Time for dinner and we would hear from Rodney, bring in fresh laundry and we would hear from Rodney, refill the water bowl and we would hear from Rodney. The wrestling match would start with the other kittens and we would hear from Rodney.

Seriously, this kitten talked a lot. He never stopped meowing or proclaiming all the things he saw and experienced around him. We heard from his forever family that their eight-year-old son would read the devotional book we gave them to Rodney. I've often wondered if Rodney talked then, too, or maybe for once he just listened.

Just as Rodney exclaimed all the happenings in his kitten world, we too can proclaim and give praise to God for all he has done.

Needing Peace

Let the peace of Christ rule in your hearts, since as members of one body you were called to peace. And be thankful.

—Colossians 3:15

What was going on with Brook? She came with six other siblings, so this was a big group. She was the smallest kitten and all black. Brook would sit far away from the play, wrestling, and even snuggling of the other kittens. Often, she would sit on a countertop, high above the action and just watch. She could be held and cuddled, but she wouldn't seek out affection.

She was a good eater. She was always the last to finish eating, cleaning up everything that the others left behind. Her tummy grew really big and round, but she didn't appear to be in pain. She was eating, drinking, and digesting well, but we could not figure out why her tummy was so big. Since she wasn't in distress, we hoped that her tiny body would eventually grow into that big tummy.

Her siblings were getting adopted, but things moved slower for Brook. She was on medication for an infection and had to finish treatment before she could be posted. There were delays with her profile posting and a request to keep her in foster care for a few more days, so Brook had lots of time as our only foster kitten.

We found that she really loved being the only kitten around and she blossomed. She showed us fun new games with her toys, she snuggled up with us on the couch for naps, and she even grew into her big tummy. She flourished when she wasn't in so much chaos.

Although life can be hectic, maybe it's important for us to be able to find peace to flourish too.

Finding You

*Then that person can pray to God
and find favor with him,
they will see God's face and shout
for joy;
he will restore them to full well-being.*

—Job 33:26

Picture a black-and-white tuxedo kitten with a cute personality named Palmer; however, he came up short in the handsome category. He did not have a well-proportioned body, was lanky, and had big ears for his head. We thought one day he would grow into those ears, but at eight weeks old, he had an awkward and gangly look. His siblings adopted quickly, and he was left with us all by himself.

He enjoyed having the new freedoms and playing the new games we gave him. He got to explore all of the house instead of just the two rooms where he grew up. Very

quickly, he taught us a new game of "Hide and Seek." It was beyond cute. He would hide around a corner and then when we came to find him, he would jump up with his front paws extended outward, then he would run to a new spot.

Then the game became more fun because we would hide around a corner and tap a toe or give a little bit of sound to indicate where we were hiding. As soon as he rounded the corner and found us, we would jump and throw our hands out wide, and he would do the same with his little front paws. Even though we both knew what was going to happen around the corner, it was always pure joy finding each other.

The delight we found in playing Palmer's game is just a fraction of the joy we will find when we see God's face and truly shout for joy. We will be filled with a happiness we never knew was possible.

Coming for You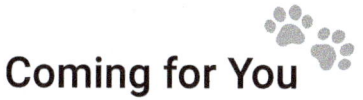

But you, LORD, do not be far from me.
You are my strength; come quickly to
help me.

—Psalm 22:19

Clinton was still waiting to be adopted. All his siblings had been chosen by their forever families, and yet no one had picked Clinton. His profile was on the website, and although there was an inquiry about him, the family had decided to adopt his brother Darien.

Clinton was still in our care, all alone, waiting not so patiently for his forever family. Clinton was also a "yeller." A yeller could be loosely defined in two ways: (1) he was an orange tabby cat, so it might be said he was "yeller" color, but (2) he also meowed a lot and loudly, as if he was always "yelling"! Clinton could not stop using his voice and meowed all the time for no specific reason.

A potential adopter saw his profile online and expressed particular interest in Clinton. She wanted to meet him, so we were telling her a little bit more about him over the phone. In the background, Clinton was, of course, meow yelling. We explained that he was extremely vocal and that she should weigh that in her adoption decision. She asked if that was him that she could hear, and we told her, "Oh, yes, that's him." She loved it!

At that moment, she yelled through the phone to Clinton, "Hang on, I'm coming for ya, baby." Right then we knew these two were a match for sure! Without seeing him, she knew there was nothing that was going to stop her from coming for this kitty!

Sometimes in life we feel like the last one, alone, but God is always seeking you. Don't be surprised when God is yelling to you, "I'm coming for ya, baby!"

www.ingramcontent.com/pod-product-compliance
Lightning Source LLC
Chambersburg PA
CBHW071203120626
46546CB00006B/2396